2016

Brian—
Happy 5th Birthday

Have fun learning abo...

Love
Grandpa and Grandma
(in Calgary and Mexico)

rs

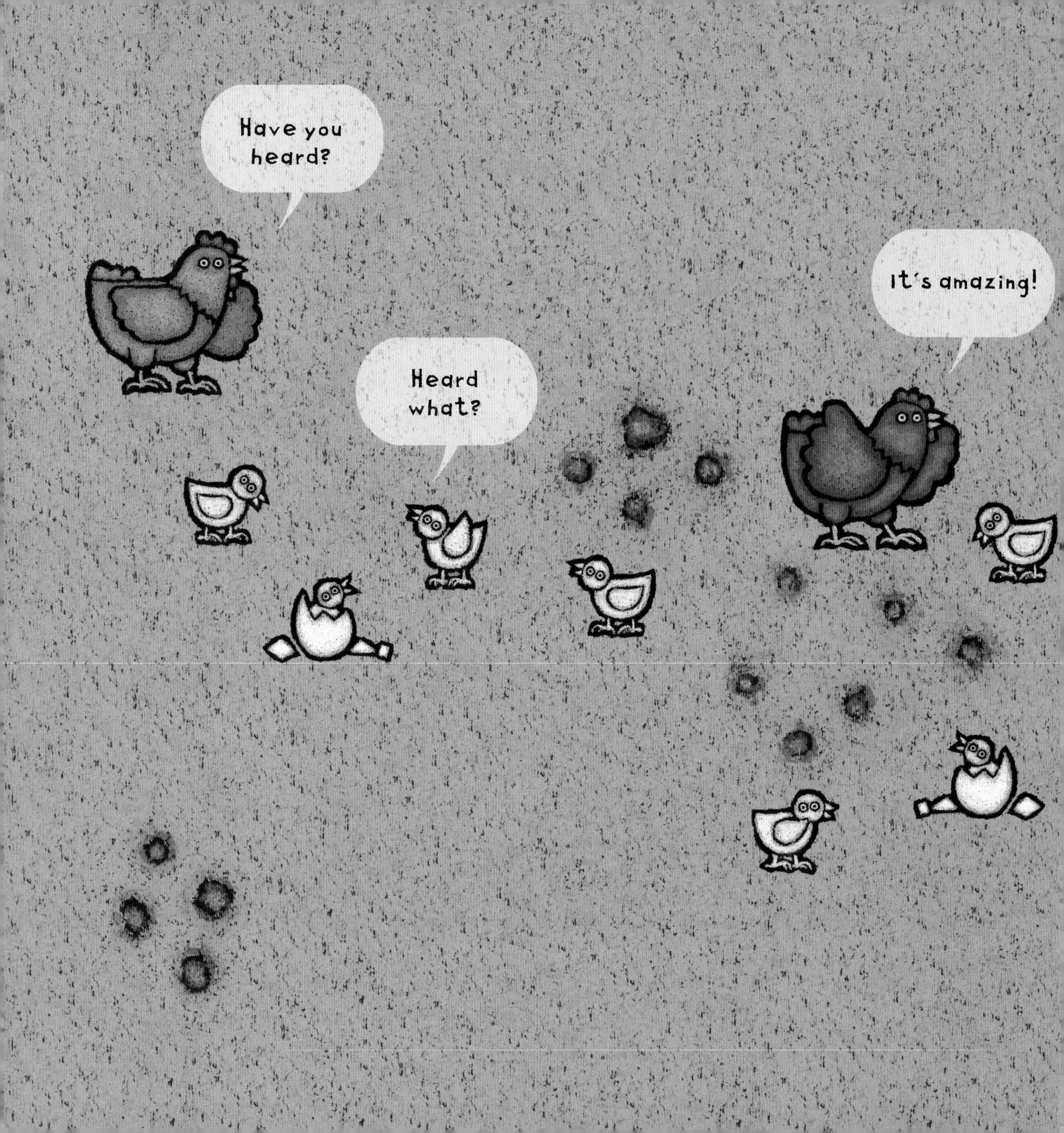
Have you heard?
Heard what?
It's amazing!

LILA PRAP
DINOSAURS?!

AMAZING NEWS, my dears! AMAZING NEWS!
I found a book on a bench behind the house
with pictures and descriptions of the
strangest animals. And you won't believe
what it says at the end of the book!
These odd-looking animals are supposed to be
our ancestors! They're called DINOSAURS!

DINOSAURS?!

Show us the
book! What else
does it say? Tell
us more!

Lila Prap (Lilijana Praprotnik Zupancic) is one of the most popular author-illustrators not only in her homeland of Slovenia but increasingly in the rest of the world. She loves to draw animals and was a nominee for the 2006 Hans Christian Andersen Award for illustration. Among her many books are *Dinosaurs?!*, *Doggie Whys*, *Cat Whys*, *Daddies* (also available in Spanish), and *Animal Lullabies*.

First published in the United States, Great Britain, Canada, Australia, and New Zealand in 2010 by NorthSouth Books Inc., an imprint of NordSüd Verlag AG, CH-8005 Zürich, Switzerland.
Paperback edition first published in Great Britiain and Australia in 2010.
This edition published in the United States in 2015 by NorthSouth Books Inc.
Distributed in the United States by NorthSouth Books Inc., New York 10016.

Library of Congress Cataloging-in-Publication Data is available.
ISBN: 978-0-7358-2284-9 (trade edition)
3 5 7 9 • 10 8 6 4 2
ISBN 978-0-7358-4022-5 (paperback edition)
3 5 7 9 • 10 8 6 4 2

Printed in China by Leo Paper Products Ltd., Heshan, Guangdong, January 2015.

www.northsouth.com

LILA PRAP

DINOSAURS?!

What does the word
DINOSAUR mean?

North
South

Why didn't they call them TERRIBLE CHICKENS if they were our ancestors?

These are not my ancestors! We never had any such strange-looking types in our family!

Are we going to turn green and grow teeth when we grow up too?

"TERRIBLE LIZARD."

Back in the old days, when people found huge bones, they thought that the bones were the remains of dragons and other fairy-tale creatures. But two hundred years ago, scientists realized that such bones belonged to a special group of reptiles that had died out. (Reptiles still alive today include crocodiles, lizards, snakes, and turtles.) Because the extinct animals were so big, scientists named them DINOSAURS, which means TERRIBLE LIZARDS. Beside bones, they found other remains that helped them figure out what these animals looked like, how they lived, and also that they were the ancestors of birds.

Our ancestors should have had beaks, I think!

One of the most fearsome dinosaurs was **TYRANNOSAURUS REX,** which means **TYRANT LIZARD KING.** It was as tall as a giraffe, as long as four cars, and as heavy as an elephant. It walked on its hind legs, and it had long teeth like knives because it was a meat eater, preying on other dinosaurs. From its footprints it was discovered that the tyrannosaur had scaly skin, like all reptiles. But nobody knows what color it was, because the colors in dinosaur skin haven't been preserved.

Why did this great-great-great-uncle of ours have such a strange collar? So he wouldn't get a cold neck?

As far as I know, he only had it because it was the fashion back then!

And why did he have three horns? Couldn't he decide which he wanted to look like, a cow or a rhino?

★ There are many dinosaur species, because they evolved over such an extremely long time. Remains have been found of dinosaurs that had jaws and teeth like lizards or crocodiles, and others whose front jaws were shaped like beaks or bills. Some of the beaked or billed dinosaurs were toothless, and some had as many as a thousand teeth toward the back of their jaws, behind the beak. The family of horned dinosaurs had parrotlike beaks used to strip leaves, and up to five horns.

If these "rhinos" had beaks, did they lay eggs too, like chickens?

TRICERATOPS, which means **THREE-HORNED FACE**, was as long as two cars put together and as heavy as five rhinos. It also walked on all fours like a rhino. Its head was bigger than a grown man's body. It was a plant eater, and it had a bony frill that was part of its skull, which protected it from being bitten by predators. Of its three horns, the longer two were larger than a seven-year-old child. It chased away its attackers with its horns, and perhaps fought with other males for females.

How big were the eggs of the largest dinosaurs? As big as a house?

I bet none of them could lay bigger and better-looking eggs than my hens!

Which came first: the egg or the dinosaur?

IKE CHICKENS!

In addition to dinosaur remains, quite a few nests with dinosaur eggs have been found. The eggs of the largest dinosaurs were not as big as you'd expect. The biggest egg ever found was about the size of a basketball. The eggs had very hard shells, making it difficult for predators to break in case the nest was left unguarded. The parents did their best to protect their nests, but they were powerless against much larger dinosaurs.

Was any dinosaur able to protect itself against the largest tyrannosaurs?

While digging up some dinosaur bones, scientists found the perfectly preserved nest of a **MAIASAURA**, or **GOOD MOTHER LIZARD**. The duck-billed maiasaura was the size of a bus. It lived in a herd, browsed on plants, and hatched its young in nests made of earth, laying thirty to forty eggs at a time, each the size of an ostrich egg. The parents took care of their young until they learned to fend for themselves, bringing them leaves they had first crushed with their thousand teeth.

Why does this one have a club on his tail? Did he whack flies with it?

He had it instead of a weight to work out with.

Or to hit himself on the head if he couldn't remember something!

GOOD PROTECTION!

Plant-eating dinosaurs protected themselves from attackers in many ways. Some were covered with spikes or hard plates. Others could only save themselves by quickly running away or by relying on protective coloring. The dinosaurs with spikes on their backs and bony tail clubs were the hardest to defeat. That is why they survived all the way to the end of the age of dinosaurs.

> My great-great-great-uncle had spikes like a hedgehog and a club on his tail? Is there any ancestor stranger than that?

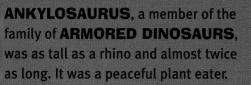

ANKYLOSAURUS, a member of the family of **ARMORED DINOSAURS**, was as tall as a rhino and almost twice as long. It was a peaceful plant eater.

As protection against predators, it had thick, armored scales on its head and spikes all over its back. Its club tail with heavy, bony knobs at the end presented

a great hazard to any attacker. With a well-aimed blow of its tail, an ankylosaurus could knock down a dinosaur larger than itself.

What are those things? Ears?

Maybe they're fans that kept them cool when it was hot.

And they had spikes on their tails to scratch with if they had an itch!

★ Scientists are always finding new dinosaur species. Sometimes it takes them years to figure out the purpose of some dinosaur body parts. When they first excavated dinosaurs with unusual growths on their backs, they presumed that these platelike growths were arranged on the dinosaurs' backs like roof tiles. Today they believe the plates were upright and perhaps helped these dinosaurs heat or cool their bodies.

> What a funny-looking great-great-great-uncle! So big but with such a tiny head!

STEGOSAURUS, meaning **ROOF LIZARD**, was the first species discovered of the large group of dinosaurs that had back plates. The stegosaur was a plant eater, and as large as two cars put together. Despite that, it had a very small head, no bigger than a large dog's. The largest plates on its back, however, were taller than a three-year-old child. It lumbered about slowly and protected itself with two large spikes on its tail.

We chickens have small heads, but we have small bodies to match.

They couldn't have been very smart! So why did they have bumps on their heads?

They probably kept bumping their heads against tree branches because they were so tall!

SMALL HEADS!

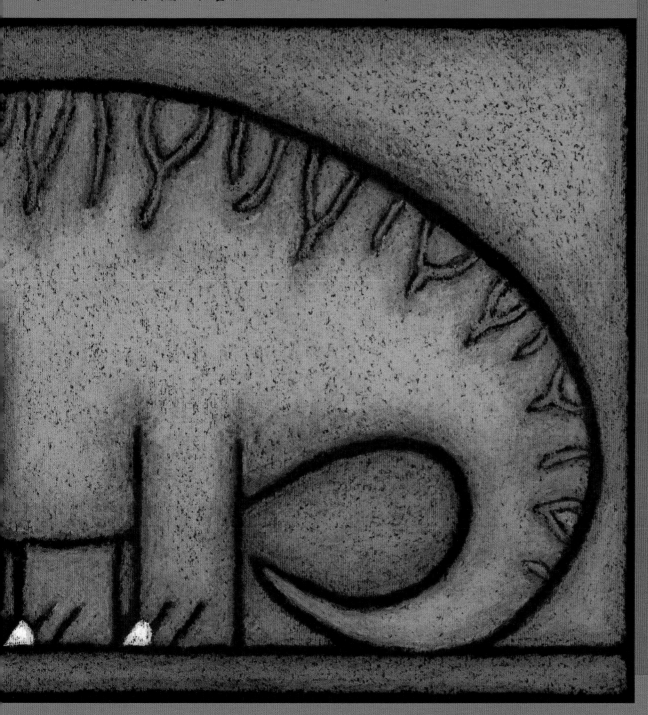

The largest dinosaurs ever discovered looked a bit like giraffes. They had long necks so they could reach the leaves on the tallest trees. With their rake-like teeth they stripped the leaves off the branches, then mashed them up in their stomachs with stones they had swallowed. In comparison to their bodies, their heads were very small indeed. There was no room for a large brain in such a small skull. But they did not really need large brains because they were so huge that no predator could attack them.

What strange ancestors! Did any others have unusual bumps on their heads?

One of the largest dinosaurs ever found is **BRACHIOSAURUS**, which means **ARM LIZARD**. It got that name because its forelimbs were longer than its hind limbs, a thing not common with dinosaurs. It was as tall as a three-story building and as heavy as ten elephants. Scientists once thought it had a breathing hole in the bump on its head that it used when wading in water, but it was later discovered that it lived on dry land.

That dome looks like hair with too much hair spray on it.

I think it looks like a cap that turned to stone because it never got washed.

Maybe their heads got thick because they were called thick-headed too many times!

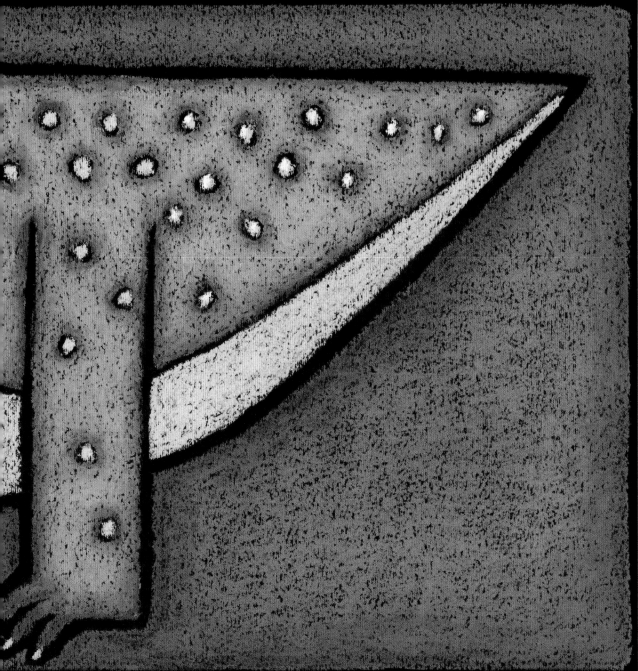

A special family of dinosaurs, the thick-headed dinosaurs, had very thick and unusually shaped skulls. Thick-headed dinosaurs varied in size. The largest were the size of a bus, with a skull as big as a washing machine and as thick as a wall. The domes on their heads were their only defense against attackers. With a strong head butt, a stegoceras could break another dinosaur's bones!

Unbelievable! Can any head look stranger than that?

STEGOCERAS, meaning **HORNED ROOF**, was the size of a horse. The top part of its skull was as thick as a brick and had a fringe of horny knobs.

Like all other thick-headed dinosaurs, the stegoceras was a plant eater and lived in a herd. When it wasn't head butting its rivals in mating contests or other battles, it browsed peacefully, tearing leaves off small trees and bushes with its sawlike teeth.

Why did this great-great-great-uncle have a stick on his head?

He must have wanted a long beak, but it grew in the wrong direction.

Or maybe he ate a stick and it got stuck in his throat!

OWTHS!

A special group of
dinosaurs, the duck-billed
dinosaurs, also had
growths on their heads.
To this day, it is not clear
what their function was.
These dinosaurs lived in
large herds near marshes.
They grazed on plants
with their bills, then ground
them up with huge numbers
of teeth on each side of
their upper and lower jaws.
They had padded hooves
instead of claws so that
they wouldn't sink into
the muddy bog.

> I can hardly
> imagine a
> funnier-looking
> head than this!

PARASAUROLOPHUS got its
name because it resembled the
SAUROLOPHUS, also known
as the **CRESTED LIZARD**. The
growth on its head looked like a hollow
stick and was as long as an adult man. This
growth was connected to its nasal cavity,
so at first scientists thought it served as a
snorkel for the dinosaur to breathe under-
water. But since the end of the tube did
not have a hole, scientists now think it made
the dinosaur's voice resonate like a horn.

What do you get when you cross a chicken with a crocodile?

A crocken. Or would that be a chickodile?

Oh, Great-great-great-grandpa, what big teeth you have!

ODILE-LIKE HEADS!

In the time of the suchomimus, wide rivers and huge marshes covered some areas of the land. There scientists discovered the remains of a dinosaur with a crocodile-like head. Its teeth and jaws were very similar to those of a present-day crocodile. Crocodiles today feed mainly on fish, so scientists think that this dinosaur also ate fish, which it caught by wading in the water.

> Were there any dinosaurs that could also swim underwater and not just wade?

SUCHOMIMUS, which means **CROCODILE MIMIC**, was as large as a tyrannosaur. It had to eat a lot of fish to fill its belly, even though some of the fish it caught were the size of cars. Suchomimus was not the only creature lurking in the rivers and lakes and preying on fish.

Relatives of present-day crocodiles lived during the same era, and they were even bigger than the suchomimus.

This one looks like a snake that has swallowed a turtle!

And then sewed a zipper onto its mouth so that the turtle couldn't escape!

Maybe it was told to zip its mouth because it talked too much!

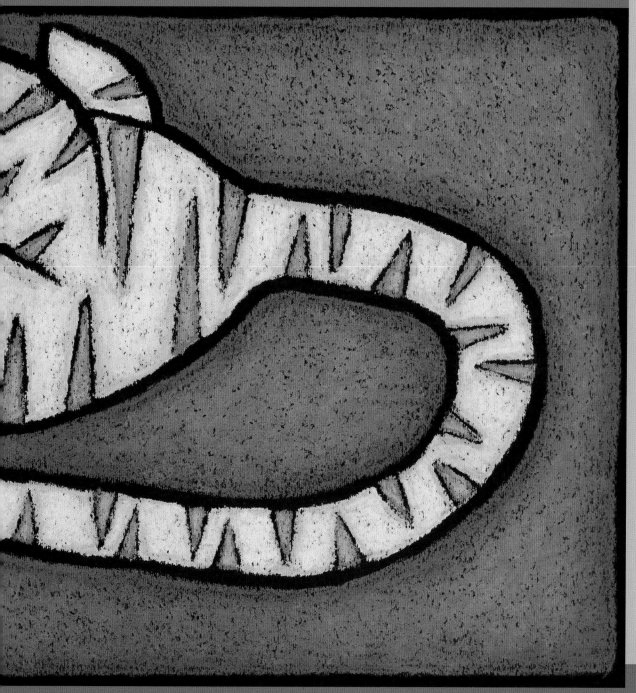

While dinosaurs ruled the land, their relatives, marine reptiles, swam the sea depths. There were also many other animals that we still know today living in the sea at that time: jellyfish, sea snails, shellfish, crabs, corals, and also many species of fish, including sharks. Marine reptiles died out at the same time as the dinosaurs. And even though some of them were huge, none surpassed the blue whale in size.

Hmm, so our great-great-great-grandparents couldn't swim, but what about the air? Who ruled the air?

he **ELASMOSAURUS**, one of the umerous sea reptiles, was as long as wo sailboats put together. It had two airs of paddle-like flippers to swim with, a small head, and a long, flexible neck. Its teeth interlocked to form a cage for any animal caught in its mouth. Unlike most dinosaurs, the elasmosaurus most probably gave birth to live young. It was too clumsy to come onto land to lay eggs.

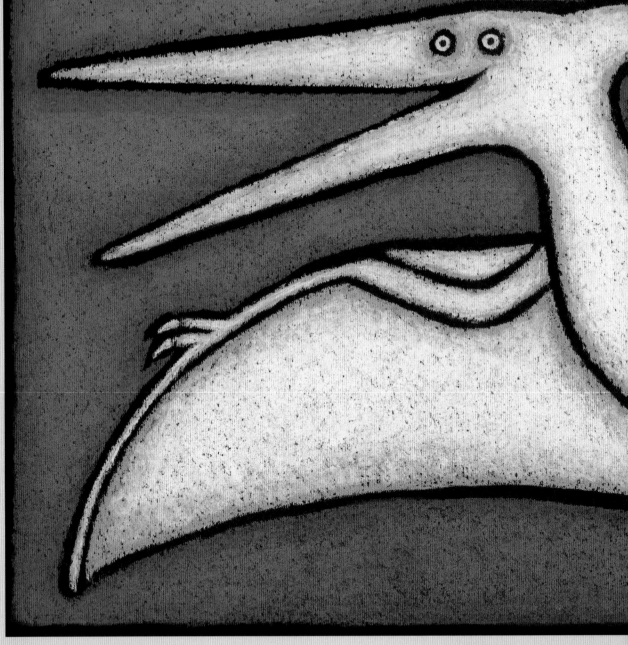

What's that growing out of the back of its head?

Maybe it wanted two beaks, one in the front and another one in the back.

Or maybe it had a propeller on its head to help it take off faster.

IES!

Long before the appearance of the first birds, winged reptiles, relatives of dinosaurs, soared above the earth. Their wings were membranes of skin, like bat wings today. Some of them were as small as sparrows. Others were larger than an airplane. The earliest flying reptiles had teeth and long tails, but later flying reptiles with shorter tails and skull crests evolved. These reptiles also died out at the same time as the dinosaurs.

Our distant relatives could fly, but dinosaurs couldn't! So what do dinosaurs have to do with birds anyway?

The **PTERANODON**, meaning **WINGED** and **TOOTHLESS**, could cover the roof of a small house if it spread its wings fully. It had a long, bony crest on its head. Scientists believe that this helped the pteranodon maintain balance when flying. The pteranodon was a fish eater. It caught fish by swooping down low and scooping up water and everything swimming in it in a skin pouch under its beak. Like pelicans do nowadays.

This one looks like a lizard playing dress up. Why did it have such huge claws on its legs?

To cut the grass, of course!

Or maybe to hook onto a branch, swing from it, and practice flying.

★ Paleontologists—that is, scientists who study the life of past geological periods—have found many clear impressions of feathers alongside skeletons of small meat-eating dinosaurs. Of all the present-day animals, only birds have feathers. On the basis of the feather impressions and other clues, scientists have concluded that dinosaurs never completely died out, as they had thought at first. On the contrary, birds evolved from one of these feathered dinosaurs.

Feathers are only one clue. I wonder what those other clues are!

VELOCIRAPTOR, or **SWIFT SEIZER**, would come up to the waist of a human adult. It was one of the most aggressive dinosaurs, and so fast that very few creatures could get away. It sank its sharp claws into its victims and tore them apart with its razor-sharp teeth. Velociraptors were most probably covered with feathers.

Scientists have discovered quill knobs on some velociraptor bones where feathers may have been attached, just as they are on birds.

If this one looks anything like me, I'm going to get a new face! Why did it have two points inside its beak?

To bite its tongue with if it said something silly!

I hope it remembered to brush and floss!

Small feathered meat-eating dinosaurs were like birds in many ways. Their bones were light, hollow, and filled with air, which is characteristic of birds, and were also similar in shape. They had feathers on their forelimbs and some other parts of the body so that they could brood eggs, just as birds do. True, they could not fly with the feathers they had, but they shared several other features with the birds of today.

> If they couldn't fly, they could only be the ancestors of ostriches, not of all birds.

OVIRAPTOR, or **EGG SEIZER**, had an unusually shaped crest on its head and two prongs on the upper palate of its beak, which it may have used to crush the shells of mollusks. It would have stood as tall as an adult human's chest. It was named by mistake: its skeleton was found on a nest of eggs that were first thought to have belonged to another dinosaur. Later it was discovered that they were the oviraptor's own eggs.

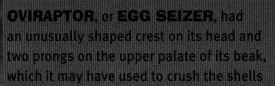

But why did they have fingers on their wings? So that they could tickle other dinosaurs?

Or wave to them as they flew past!

Why don't we have teeth? Did dinosaurs forget to brush?

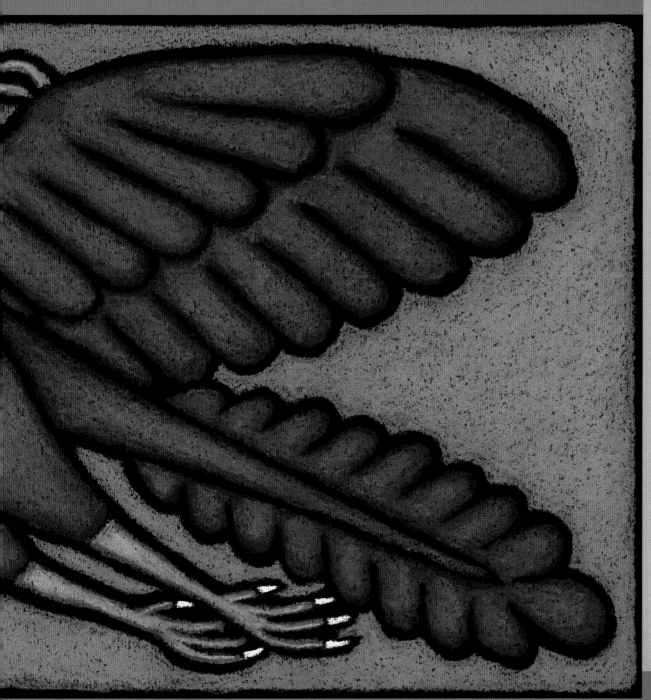

More than a hundred years ago the remains of an animal that resembled both a bird and a dinosaur were found. Its skeleton was like a dinosaur's, and its wings were like a bird's. It had a feathered body and flight feathers that enabled it to glide. All modern-day birds evolved from ancestors like this half bird, half dinosaur. So the descendants of the dinosaurs who learned to fly still live all around us. And because chickens are birds, their ancestors are dinosaurs too.

From now on my name is Chickesaurus Rex!

ARCHAEOPTERYX, or **ANCIENT BIRD**, is the earliest known bird. It evolved at a time when the largest dinosaurs roamed the land and the largest flying reptiles flew in the skies. Archaeopteryx is a descendant of a small meat-eating dinosaur. Unlike the birds of today, it had a jaw with teeth, very strong claws, and a long, bony tail.

In birds, the jaw changed into a beak, and all the parts that made flying difficult (such as teeth, bony tails, and wing claws) disappeared.

There's another thing scientists have discovered. At the time dinosaurs ruled the earth, some small, mouselike creatures appeared, and from them all modern-day mammals evolved. Mammals are beings that give birth to live young that suckle milk: elephants, monkeys and apes, cows, horses, dogs, cats, foxes, and many more. Even people, who have existed only one-hundredth of the time since the age of the dinosaurs, evolved from this same mousy ancestor!

I knew it! I knew I was something special! A descendant of the mightiest beings that ever walked the earth! Born to rule! Even the sun doesn't rise until I crow with my dinosaur voice!

They've been stealing eggs from us for too long.

They better not call us chicken! We come from dinosaurs!

RELATIVES OF DINOSAURS
MARINE REPTILES

DINOSAURS, o
Only the dinosaurs and other reptiles
There were also many other dinosaur

ELASMOSAURUS
85 to 65 million years ago

> Here you can see how closely related these dinosaurs were to one another!

SUCHOMIMUS
125 to 112 million years ago

ARCHAEOPTERYX
150 to 145 million
years ago

BRACHIOSAURU
150 to 145 million ye

VELOCIRAPTOR
75 to 70 million
years ago

OVIRAPTOR
75 million
years ago

> And they have all died out except us! It's lucky that my ancestors had children, who then had children, who then had children . . . or I wouldn't have hatched today!

All modern-day birds, including CHICKENS

TYRANNOSAURUS REX
68 to 65 million years ago

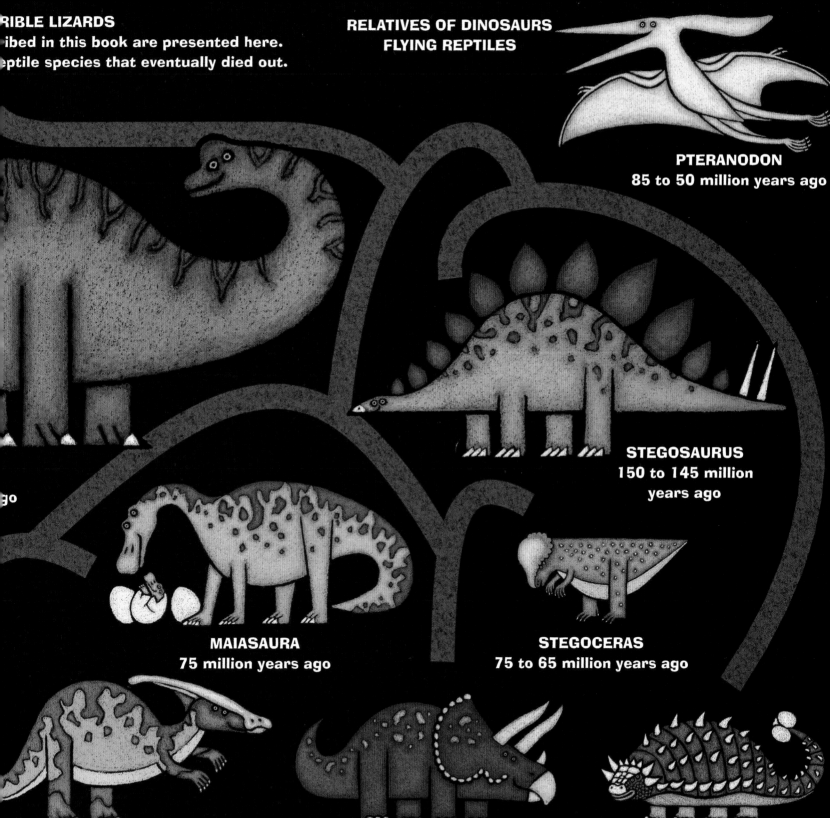

RIBLE LIZARDS
ibed in this book are presented here.
eptile species that eventually died out.

**RELATIVES OF DINOSAURS
FLYING REPTILES**

PTERANODON
85 to 50 million years ago

STEGOSAURUS
150 to 145 million
years ago

go

MAIASAURA
75 million years ago

STEGOCERAS
75 to 65 million years ago

PARASAUROLOPHUS
76 to 73 million years ago

TRICERATOPS
70 to 65 million years ago

ANKYLOSAURUS
70 to 65 million years ago